The Growth Seeker's Handbook

Strategies for Continuous Improvement

Table of Contents

There is only one corner of the universe you can be certain of improving, and that's your own self.

Chapter 1. Introduction

Set sails on a transformative journey towards relentless growth and continuous improvement with our Special Report, "The Growth Seeker's Handbook: Strategies for Continuous Improvement". Discover an array of enlightening strategies that act as a compass, guiding you towards your personal and professional development. This report isn't about high-end algorithms or complex calculus equations. It's about you — your ambitions, your aspirations, your growth potential. We've painted it in the vibrant colors of relatable stories, lit it with the sparks of wisdom, and sprinkled it with thought-provoking insights. Providing both pragmatic points and inspiring anecdotes, this report is your resource to undertake a ride of growth against the tides of complacency. Be it a seasoned professional or someone just starting out in their career, this milestone guide fosters the spirit of continuous learning and improvement. Just a glance at this report, and you'll find the seeds of your next big leap, ready to be sown!

Chapter 2. Understanding the Growth Seeker's Mindset

To get the wheels of growth and progress spinning at their fastest, it is vital to first understand the mindset of a growth seeker. Let's embark on this voyage of discovery through the core of the growth-seeking mindset.

2.1. Understanding the Core

One must be aware that 'growth' is a vast and complex concept, encompassing a variety of aspects. Development can occur in diverse fields and domains, be it personal or professional. However, when these diverse forms of growth are interspersed, they lead to a compelling compound effect. The essence of growth-seeking is not confined to a single domain but encapsulates a bundle of improvements and enhancements across multiple spheres of life.

2.2. The Cornerstone of Growth

At the cornerstone of this growth-seeking mindset nestles a deep-seated belief — the belief in one's capability for constant and consistent improvement and development. It is accompanied by an unwavering commitment to constructively utilize one's potential. This belief is nurtured by an inner dialogue that recurrently asks: Can I be better at what I do? As a growth seeker, the answer would always echo a resounding 'yes'. You become engaged in an ongoing quest for betterment, an unceasing endeavor to continue learning and enhancing, propelling an upward spiral of constant growth.

2.3. Embracing Adaptability and Flexibility

In the world we inhabit, change is the only constant. Novel situations, new challenges, and unexpected hurdles present themselves incessantly. A quintessential feature of the growth seeker's mindset is the readiness to adapt and embrace change. Adaptability stems from openness to learn, unlearn, and relearn. Flexibility to modify existing beliefs and methods in light of new information or changing circumstances sets the stage for relentless growth and improvement.

2.4. The Power of Curiosity and Open-mindedness

Curiosity, the desire to know more, to understand better, and to explore further, is like the fuel that powers the engine of growth. When combined with an open mind, curiosity becomes a potent catalyst to propel you towards your development goals. Open-mindedness here dictates a willingness to consider different viewpoints and perspectives. It's about questioning your assumptions, challenging your beliefs, and being open to evidence that contradicts your current understanding. This practice fosters in you the traits of a truly enthusiastic learner, who ceaselessly seeks opportunities for growth.

2.5. Relishing Challenges

Growth and comfort are often found at opposite ends of the spectrum. Therefore, a desire to seek and take on challenges is another characteristic feature of the growth-seeking mindset. Challenges tend to push us out of our comfort zone, and that is precisely where growth happens. Such an attitude not only helps us overcome difficulties but also turns them into stepping stones for growth and development. Seeing every challenge as an opportunity forms the backbone of the growth seeker's mindset.

2.6. Celebrating Failures

Failure is often stigmatized, seen has a sign of inadequacy or incompetence. However, individuals possessing a growth mindset view failure differently. Instead of fixating on the negative fallout, they see failure as an opportunity to learn, improve, and grow. Thus, celebrating failures, not as an end but as the beginning of a new journey towards success, is integral to the growth-seeking mindset.

2.7. Practicing Self-reflection

Critical and regular self-reflection forms the last mosaic piece in forming a comprehensive understanding of the growth-seeking mindset. Reflection allows you to discern your strengths and weaknesses, appreciate your accomplishments, and identify areas where improvement is needed. It's a way to hold yourself accountable, to introspect on your actions and their consequences, and to align your future actions with your growth and development goals.

The journey to embracing the growth-seeker's mindset may not always be smooth. It requires you to experiment, take calculated risks, face failures, and embrace challenges. But with the right mindset, consistent effort, and an unwavering commitment, you're sure to carve out a pathway leading to relentless growth and continued improvement. The road might stretch into the distant horizon, with bends and curves along the way, but the treasure at the end, the treasure of growth and self-fulfillment, is worth every step.

Chapter 3. The Imperative of Continuous Learning

Continued enlightenment permits you to peel back the illusory veil of knowledge, revealing the world in its natural kaleidoscope of curiosity and intrigue. It sets the stage for endless change and growth, pushing boundaries across personal and professional dominions. It is not the mere acquisition of facts, but the exploration of their interconnectedness, the understanding of their application, and the contemplation of their obscured intricacies. An eternal student of life, the growth seeker, thus, is moored in the bedrock of continuous learning.

3.1. The Rationale Behind Continuous Learning

Understanding the 'why' behind continuous learning is pivotal. It throws light upon the urgency and necessity of this incessant quest for knowledge. The world as we know it is evolving at a breakneck pace. Every day, innovative technologies, creative ideas, and transformative developments emerge on the global stage. Complacency leads to stagnation, while continuous learning ensures one stays afloat, buoyant in this rushing river of information.

Learning catalyzes personal and professional development, often resulting in elevated self-confidence, expanded skill set, and a motivated disposition. Life's vicissitudes become arenas for learning, urging the learner to probe deeper, question further, and understand better. Cognitive agility is rewarded, while the thirst for knowledge is ceaselessly stoked.

3.2. Bridging the Gap: From Learning to Unlearning and Relearning

The process of learning is often viewed as linear. However, this is far from the truth. Part of continuous learning is unlearning obsolete facts and theories. Misconceptions and half-truths are discarded, making way for veritable knowledge. This unlearning clears the cobwebs of dogma that may obscure vision and stunts intellectual growth.

Relearning is equally significant. It entails revisiting past knowledge to inculcate deeper understanding, refine concepts, or correct possible misinterpretations. In this cyclical process of learning, unlearning, and relearning lies the path to growth and continuous improvement.

3.3. Lifelong Learning: The Soul of Personal and Professional Growth

Lifelong learning is an ongoing, proactive, self-motivated pursuit of knowledge that can enrich personal and professional life. It infuses our lives with purpose, offering us novel perspectives and ideas, thus developing a well-rounded personality. Lifelong learners continuously strive for self-improvement, engage in introspection, and embrace self-directed learning. They seize learning opportunities that lies in everyday encounters, conversations, and experiences.

In the realm of professional growth, lifelong learning comes to the forefront. Organizations that nurture a learning culture are poised to adapt, innovate, and lead. The employees who adopt a growth mindset actively participate in continuous skill improvement, thus contributing towards organizational success while ascending their career ladder.

3.4. Tools and Techniques for Nurtifying Continuous Learning

Nourishment of continuous learning calls upon certain tools and strategies. Reading, a classic learning tool, aids in exploring diverse perspectives, exposes us to innovative ideas, and refines our understanding of the world and its myriad nuances.

Technological advancements like e-learning platforms, online courses, webinars, and podcasts bring a trove of knowledge to the learner's fingertips. It revolutionizes learning, demolishing geographic boundaries and allowing individuals to learn at their own pace.

Reflective practices such as journaling, conducting self-assessments, and engaging in thoughtful discussions help consolidate learning. Such practices foster critical thinking, highlight areas of improvement, and stimulate intellectual growth.

3.5. Cultivating a Learning Mindset

Cultivating a learning mindset implies maintaining an open, non-judgmental, inquisitive stance towards life. It involves recognizing the limits of our knowledge, cherishing intellectual humility, and fostering the courage to probe the unknown.

Continuous learning is never comfortable, as it challenges ingrained beliefs and assumptions. Courage to face discomfort and resilience in the face of setbacks are the quintessence of a learning mindset.

In the grand narrative of growth, the role of continuous learning is unparalleled. It is the lifeblood of personal and professional development, opening doors to unnoticed pathways, catalyzing change, and fueling relentless growth. Growth isn't a destination but an endless journey, and continuous learning is the steadfast compass guiding this voyage toward unfathomable greatness.

Chapter 4. Transforming Challenges into Opportunities

Our expedition into the landscapes of growth and improvement wouldn't be complete without taking a detour to provide you with a comprehensive understanding of one of life's most fundamental principles - the principle of transforming challenges into opportunities. This chapter is not just a theoretical exposition; it serves as a roadmap filled with tools and tactics for turning adversity into an ally.

4.1. Embracing Challenges: The Initial Step Towards Growth

The genesis of any transformative journey comes when we learn to see challenges not as roadblocks, but as catalysts in our growth journey. This switch in perception is as critical as it is transformative. It's as though we've been using powerful binoculars, but only now do we adjust the focus, allowing us to view our surroundings clearly. We often confront obstacles and setbacks with aversion, but the reality is that they help us step out of our comfort zones, uniquely qualifying them to catalyze our growth.

By reshaping our perspective, we give ourselves a refreshing vision - a new set of lenses through which we can see life's adversities as a crucial part of our existence which are meant not to break us, but to make us.

4.2. The Ingredients of Transformation: Persistence, Patience, and Perspective

Just as a chef requires several ingredients to create a culinary masterpiece, our journey of transforming challenges into opportunities necessitates a mix of persistence, patience, and perspective.

Persistence is the element that pushes us through despite the odds. It's the force that propels us over obstacles and keeps us moving when the road gets tough. It's the refusal to quit, the determination to keep going, despite countervailing circumstances.

Patience, on the other hand, is an equally crucial ingredient that we need to exercise when we fail to see immediate results. It's the compass that guides us when the darkness of uncertainty looms large. It helps us hold steady in the face of adversity, affording us the necessary time for growth and self-reflection.

Finally, **perspective** is the ability to view situations from multiple angles and to choose the one that aligns with our growth and improvement. It reframes our mindset and recalibrates our approach to failure and adversity, positioning us to stumble upon opportunities where others see only roadblocks.

4.3. Utilize Failure as Fertilizer: Cultivating a Growth Mindset

Often perceived negatively, failure is, in reality, a powerful stimulus for growth. By examining our failures, we can identify our shortcomings and reframe them into learning opportunities, transforming the barren soil of defeat into a fertile land of potential growth. For this process to unfold, we need a growth mindset - an understanding that abilities can be developed, failures can be a stepping stones to success, and difficulties are merely disguised opportunities.

4.4. The Art of Positivity: Cultivating Optimism in the Face of Adversity

Keeping a positive attitude in the face of adversity is like carrying a lantern in the depths of a dark forest; it illuminates the path and dispels fear. Optimism breathes life into the tires of our persistence and keeps us fuelled as we journey along the rocky road of transformation. It's the permite that allows us to scan through the fog of uncertainty and spot the rainbow of possibilities.

4.5. Conclusion: The Merit of Challenges

In conclusion, challenges are not to be dreaded or avoided, but rather embraced and appreciated. They are the chisels that shape us, the furnace that tempers our spirit, and the weight that strengthens our resolve. By treating challenges as opportunities, we unlock a whole new world of possibilities for growth and improvement. This understanding is the true essence of transforming challenges into opportunities, a process that, once mastered, will serve as a pillar for continuous personal and professional development.

Combining these principles, practicing patience, persistence, and maintaining a positive perspective, we can turn every challenge into an instrument of unrivaled growth. Thus, misequipped, we are standing on the threshold of a radical transformation that will propel us towards relentless growth and continuous improvement. So let's set sail and embark on this journey together, turning every stumble into a stride and every trial into triumph!

Chapter 5. The Role of Curiosity in Growth

Curiosity, the thirst for exploring unfamiliar territories and asking novel questions, serves as a potent driving force for growth in multiple dimensions. Viewed as an intrinsic human trait, curiosity propels us beyond the realm of comfort, enabling us to innovate, acquire new knowledge, and expand the range of our competencies. Essentially, curiosity gifts us tickets to embark upon the journey of constant learning and improvement, nudging us towards growth stages otherwise untouched and unvisited.

5.1. The Interconnection of Curiosity and Growth

Commence this exploration by understanding the dynamic interconnection of curiosity and growth. Curiosity can be deemed as the seed that gives life to the tree of personal and professional experiences which, in turn, catapult us towards exponential growth. Considering curiosity as a mindset, it transcends into liberating individuals from the shackles of limited perspectives, which is a pivotal aspect for personal growth.

Curiosity motivates us to engage in robust information-seeking behavior, vicariously blending the relationship between knowledge accumulation and skill improvement. As a result, it augments personal growth.

From a professional standpoint, curiosity facilitates the fostering of a culture of innovation and originality. Driven by the desire to probe and explore leads to developing solutions, process enhancements, and novel ideas that can contribute significantly to professional growth.

5.2. The Psychology of Curiosity

Penetrating the psychological realm of curiosity uncovers its strong ties with the innate human desire for learning. Endless queries, insatiable thirst for knowledge, and an enormous appetite for diving into the depths of mystery - these, fundamentally, are what define a curious personality.

Delving deeper into this intricate relationship, scientific research supports that curiosity enhances cognitive processes, learning abilities, problem-solving skills, and overall intellectual growth. Chiefly, it promotes active learning, where individuals grasp concepts more effectively and hold onto information for more extended periods.

It also leads to exploring both linear and lateral thinking spaces, thereby broadening the range of solutions to a given problem or challenge. This pattern of divergent thinking, triggered by curiosity, fuels creative and constructive thought processes, resulting in optimal decision-making and ideation.

5.3. Cultivating Curiosity for Learning and Development

Owning a curiosity-engineered mindset is no less than an investment channelled towards continuous learning and development. This focus on learning allows us to construct meaningful relationships with our surroundings. Here's how one could cultivate curiosity to nurture growth:

1. Embrace uncertainty: Let go of fear and apprehensions associated with the uncertain. Remember, questions propel curiosity, so stay open to stepping into the unknown.

2. Engage in active learning: Learn by doing. Experiential learning

is an excellent way to stimulate curiosity and also allows for immediate feedback and improvements.

3. Foster diversity: Connect with diverse people, ideas, cultures, and perspectives. It not only enriches knowledge but heightens cognition.

4. Practice 'Why?' and 'What if?': Channelize toward the habit of questioning. Both 'Why?' and 'What if?' are powerful questions that can trigger deep insights and novel ideas.

5. Engage in critical thinking: Dissociate from the surface level and engage in depth. Critical thinking urges us to examine premises, question their validity, and logically interpret the impact of an action or decision.

5.4. Curiosity: A Leverage for Professional Growth

The linkage between curiosity and professional growth is undeniable. In an organizational context, curiosity promotes an environment brimming with ideas, solutions, and enhancements.

By sparking questions, curiosity triggers innovation. It can lead to better problem-solving abilities, efficient coping mechanisms, resilience, and increased job satisfaction. Curiosity leads to the generation and acceptance of diverse ideas, collaboratively fueling creativity and fostering a dynamic, progressive work culture.

Nurturing curiosity allows professionals to stay ahead of industry trends, anticipate changes, and adapt to emerging scenarios. Thus, it becomes crucial to developing professional competencies, enhancing leadership skills, encouraging team collaboration, and maintaining a competitive edge in today's fast-paced business environment.

Remember, curiosity is the fuel for growth. Keep questioning, stay inspired, and let the passion for exploring the unknown guide your journey towards relentless growth. Embrace curiosity, continually learn, and persistently improve — the universe of knowledge and growth is vast and endlessly fascinating.

Chapter 6. Creating a Personal Strategy for Improvement

In the pursuit of growth, it is essential to have a strategy, a roadmap that guides your decisions and actions. A personal strategy for improvement is a comprehensive yet flexible plan that details your objectives and the means to achieve them, dominated by practical measures designed to foster continuous growth. In this chapter, we take a winding journey, navigating through the steps in developing a unique strategy tailored to your aspirations.

6.1. Understanding Your Current Situation

At the outset, comprehension of your current situation forms the cornerstone of creating a personal improvement strategy. Barely anyone can plan a journey without knowing their starting point. This understanding involves an honest self-evaluation of your skills, knowledge, strengths, and areas that need enhancement. Obtaining clear insights can be accomplished through various self-assessment methods such as SWOT analysis, vision and goal setting practices, and seeking feedback from others.

6.2. Setting Your Goals

The next crucial step is setting your goals. Ideally, these should be SMART: Specific, Measurable, Attainable, Relevant, and Time-bound. Articulate them clearly, writing them down, as the act of writing makes your intentions tangible and less likely to be forgotten or discarded. Convince yourself why these targets are essential for your personal and professional growth and make a mental note of these reasons. Let these goals be your touchstone, keeping you focused and motivated on the road to improvement.

6.3. Identifying and Leveraging Your Strengths

Recognizing your existing strengths is a powerful tool. It helps you determine where you stand and defines the basis upon which you can build. Every significant improvement strategy leverages and amplifies strengths first before turning attention to weaker areas.

6.4. Acknowledging and Working on Your Weaknesses

Everyone has areas of weakness. Acknowledging these is not defeatist; rather, it's a trademark of someone forward-thinking, willing to improve. The key here is not simply to gloss over weaknesses, but to address them head-on, weaving into your strategy plans for focused improvement on these fronts.

6.5. Developing Skills and Knowledge

As the global landscape is continuously evolving, staying proactive in developing skills and knowledge base is non-negotiable. Identify the abilities and knowledge areas necessary for your future growth and design a plan to acquire them, involving various sources like online courses, books, or mentors.

6.6. Embracing Change

In the ever-changing world we live in, embracing change is indispensable for growth. Equip yourself to adapt to new circumstances with resilience and enthusiasm, treating each shift as an opportunity to move forward.

6.7. Tracking Progress

Reference points help assess growth and make necessary adjustments. Set milestone markers along your improvement journey, not only to keep track of progress but also to celebrate small victories.

6.8. Staying Consistent

Lastly, remember that consistency is vital. Discouragement may come when desired results are not immediate, yet it's important to understand that incremental changes often lead to massive transformations. Keep going, fueled by the belief in your potential and the validity of your ambitions.

Creating a personal strategy for improvement isn't a one-off measure, but a perpetual commitment to an evolving process attuned to change and open to revisions. As you traverse through your growth story, this strategy becomes your steady companion, providing direction and clearing confusions. It enables you to make the best use of your abilities and resources, fostering continuous and effective self-improvement. Remember, steadfastness in your pursuit, adaptability to change, consistency in action, and tenacity despite adversities are your strongest allies. Your strategy is your beacon of light, illuminating the path to unending growth and relentless improvement.

Chapter 7. Get Comfortable with Being Uncomfortable: Tactics for Embracing Change

There's a universal truth that often goes overlooked in our pursuit of success: discomfort breeds growth. It's an oddly comforting thought, yet striving to stay in our comfort zones often muffles the real promise of progress. It is within this unfamiliar territory — where tension stirs and anxious butterflies flutter — that we truly evolve.

7.1. Embracing the Zone of Discomfort

What lies beyond the comfort zone? It's a realm laden with uncertainties, laden with newer experiences, and character-building challenges. It's a place where resilience is both demanded and nurtured. Venturing into this realm fosters a shift in perspective, changing the way we perceive challenges. It bolsters our ability to adapt and innovate, effectively reshaping our erstwhile complacency into a proactive pursuit of growth.

Stepping out of the comfort zone can bring a wave of apprehension, but such moments house an opportunity for character development. Though discomfort has a somewhat negative connotation, it's important to reframe our understanding of it. It is not about courting unnecessary stress or anxiety, but about courageously stepping into new experiences with grit, persistence, and a dash of curiosity.

7.2. Understanding the Uncomfortable: Identifying Growth-Inducing Discomfort

The first step towards this radical shift lies in understanding the nature of discomfort. Not all discomfort leads to growth, and discerning the difference between growth-inducing discomfort and simply detrimental stress is essential. Growth-inducing discomfort arises from experiences that challenge our current capabilities but don't completely overwhelm us, like taking on a complex project at work or learning a new skill. These situations push us to broaden our limits and acquire new competencies.

7.3. Methods to Embrace the Uncomfortable

Post identification, embracing discomfort requires intentional strategy. Here are a few methods to aid you:

1. **Practice makes comfort**: Making small, incremental challenges part of our routines helps usher in the unfamiliar more seamlessly. Begin with something as simple as adopting a new hobby and progressively increase the challenge.

2. **Think growth**: Abandon the notion of 'instant perfection'. Instead, celebrate every bit of progress on the road to mastery.

3. **Mindful actions**: Practicing mindfulness aids in monitoring our reactions to discomfort. It encourages self-analysis and adjustment, fostering a growth-centric mindset.

4. **Leverage support systems**: Social support, be it friends, family, or mentors, can be instrumental in managing discomfort during the initial phases of stepping out from our comfort zones.

7.4. Give up the Fear of Failure

Equally vital is dealing with the fear of failure. It is natural to equate success with comfort, but the true legends of progress often tell a different tale. Embracing a 'learn-from-failure' mentality mitigates the fear and, in turn, eases the discomfort of trying something new. Treat every failure as an opportunity to get back up, re-calibrate, and move forward.

7.5. The Uncomfortable is the New Normal

As you embark on this journey of engaging with discomfort and inviting growth, bear in mind that the uncomfortable will become your new normal. Each step outside your comfort zone expands it, turns intimidating prospects into everyday routines. Over time, this cumulative courage results in transformative personal and professional development.

In the grand scheme, the euphoria of success and self-improvement vastly outweighs the initial discomfort. Therefore, get comfortable with being uncomfortable, not because it's easy or always pleasurable, but because it's the most reliable path towards growth.

Chapter 8. The Ongoing Conversation: Feedback as a Catalyst for Growth

Feedback: often dreaded, yet crucial in our journey of continuous growth and improvement. It serves as a mirror, reflecting our strengths and the areas we need to work on as we strive towards personal and professional development. It begins with grasping the essence of feedback and developing a mindset to accept it positively, harnessing it as a tool for advancement rather than a weapon of criticism.

8.1. Understanding Feedback

Feedback is the information we receive regarding our behavior, actions, or performance. It can come from an external source such as a colleague, mentor, or client, or internally through self-evaluation. Assessing the effect and impact we have on our surroundings or the job we perform, feedback, when utilized appropriately, can steer us towards improvement.

However, accepting feedback is not an easy task. It often brings discomfort, raising defences that can blind us to the lessons it offers. This reaction stems from our innate preference for positive appreciation and our fear of negative criticism. The key lies in shifting our perspective of feedback from an attack on our ego to a catalyst for our growth. Once this shift happens, feedback becomes a valuable tool to unlock our potential, escalate productivity, and enhance our personal and professional relationships.

8.2. The Power of Feedback

Feedback has immense power to steer us towards improvement. Constructive criticism can be an effective motivator, encouraging us to rectify our deficiencies and empower our strengths. Furthermore, it fosters a culture of openness, transparency, and mutual respect among teams, driving collective improvement. Positive feedback boosts self-esteem and motivation, while critical feedback, when presented constructively, can present opportunities to evolve and progress.

Moreover, regular feedback allows for adjustments in behavior, ideas, or our approach to tasks before they morph into bigger issues. Regular performance reviews and self-evaluation keep us aligned with our goals and cognitive of our growth trajectory. In essence, feedback fuels us to continually hone our skills and grow as professionals and individuals.

8.3. The Art of Giving and Receiving Feedback

Receiving feedback is one facet of the equation while giving it completes the picture. The process of giving feedback is equally critical for the giver and the receiver. Keeping a few principles in mind can ensure that the feedback given is productive and well received.

When offering feedback, the focus should be on clarity and specificity. Statements should be based on observed behaviors and communicated in a manner that is constructive, honest, and non-judgmental. Feedback should be timely to ensure its relevance and the recipient's capacity to implement changes. The intent of feedback should be developmental, directing towards growth and improvement.

Furthermore, in a professional setting, 360-degree feedback (incorporating feedback from all levels within an organization) can provide a holistic view of an individual's performance and areas of improvement. This comprehensive, round-robin method of feedback offers a more balanced perspective and promotes a culture of trust.

On the other side, receiving feedback also requires skill. One needs to keep an open mind, try not to take the feedback personally, respond rather than react, and make sure to act upon it. A receptive attitude towards feedback, coupled with a genuine willingness to improve, is key to personal and professional growth.

8.4. Growth through Feedback - Case Study

Consider the story of Tom, an enthusiastic and hardworking employee at a thriving software company. He comes to work each day with a positive attitude, ready to tackle new challenges. However, he often keeps to himself, prefers working alone, and has difficulties in team coordination.

During his annual feedback session, his manager highlights these tendencies and offers constructive feedback regarding his need to improve his teamwork skills. The manager gives specific examples of where Tom's solitary working affected project deadlines, and also praises his positive attributes such as his dedication to work and innovative thought process.

While initially defensive, Tom then takes a step back and reevaluates the feedback. He realizes that by making adjustments to his approach, he can become a more valuable team player and make a more significant impact on project successes.

In this scenario, feedback proved to be a catalyst for Tom's growth. It pushed him outside his comfort zone, leading him to identify and work on his shortcomings, enhancing his team player skill-set.

In conclusion, turning feedback into a stepping-stone for growth involves reinforcing a positive mindset, understanding the importance of feedback, mastering the art of giving and receiving feedback, and continually striving for improvement. This ongoing conversation of feedback, when harnessed correctly, truly becomes a catalyst for unceasing growth and development, propelling us towards our ultimate goals. Remember, each piece of feedback you receive or give is a golden opportunity for you and others to grow. Embrace it, learn from it, act on it, and watch the transformation unfold.

Chapter 9. Charting Progress: Effective Methods for Tracking Your Growth Journey

The journey of growth is a long and winding road. One must learn how to chart one's progress, carefully marking milestones and taking note of setbacks to leverage them as stepping stones to success. It's not just about pulling oneself forward undeterred, but also about periodically assessing where one stands vis-a-vis where one started from and ultimately, where one wants to be.

9.1. Unpacking the Importance of Assessing Progress

Regular assessment of one's growth and progress is akin to charting the path for a journey. It helps identify the distance traveled, the obstacles encountered, and the progress earned. Such assessments provide valuable insights allowing one to calibrate their efforts and refine their strategies while keeping in sight the final destination.

Just as a traveler on an extensive road trip relies on a map or a GPS system, your personal growth journey necessitates a comprehensive, yet flexible, means of tracking progress. A well-delineated roadmap not only acknowledges your triumphs and corrects your path as required, but also elucidates the ground yet to be covered.

9.2. The Art of Meaningful Self-Evaluation

Self-evaluation is pivotal to track progress. It cultivates an awareness about the self that breeds growth. It's crucial to incorporate a careful, honest analysis of your achievements, struggles, and stagnations.

To succeed with self-evaluation: - Set clear, achievable metrics against which you can measure your growth. These could be based on skill attainment, knowledge acquisition, attitude or behavioral changes, advancements in personal relationships, or progress in career goals. - Develop a ritual around self-evaluation. Designating specific time for reflection can prime your mindset for honest and constructive self-assessment. - Journaling can be a powerful tool for reflecting on your growth journey. Record victories, setbacks, and insights. Captured in words, these became tangible milestones guiding your path. - Cultivate a growth mindset that values progress over perfection. It's a journey, after all!

9.3. Achieving Accountability with Progress Tracking Tools

With the advent of technology, numerous tools and techniques are available that can help document and visualize progress. These tools serve as accountability partners, nudging you when needed and keeping your momentum steady. They range from digital applications that help monitor performance in various areas to traditional pen-and-paper methods that provide a tangibility to your growth journey.

Here are a few effective tools to consider: - Digital applications: Many apps allow for the tracking of habits, goals, and milestones. Applications such as Habitica, Strides, or Lifetick can help track various aspects of your life, from health and wellness, to professional skill development, to personal habit formation. - Goal-setting frameworks: The OKR (Objectives and Key Results) framework, originally developed at Intel and popularized by Google, can be a powerful method for setting and tracking personal goals. In this framework, you establish major Objectives (what you want to achieve) and Key Results (specific, measurable actions that lead you towards each objective). - Traditional journaling: The act of noting down your progress, thoughts, and reflections provide a tangible sense of progress. Plus, it can be therapeutic and introspective. - Vision boards: They allow you to visualize your goals and progress. By creating a physical or digital collage of images, pictures, and affirmations of your dreams and aspirations, you can foster motivation and positive feelings.

9.4. Harnessing the Power of Feedback

One key aspect often overlooked in the process of tracking progress is feedback. Constructive feedback from trusted peers, mentors, or coaches can offer an external perspective to complement your self-assessment. By aligning this external perspective with your self-evaluation, you can gain a comprehensive understanding of your growth trajectory.

To make feedback work for you: - Cultivate a mentally open space where you can listen, understand, and react constructively to feedback. - Develop relationships and networking skills to find mentors or peers who can provide meaningful feedback. - Learn to ask the right questions to probe for helpful insights.

9.5. Celebrating Progress and Learning from Losses

Success can be a powerful motivator. Celebrating every milestone, however small, can contribute to maintaining a positive growth mindset. Rewarding your accomplishments enforces the belief that your efforts are yielding results.

But, growth isn't always linear. Setbacks and stalling are also part of your journey. In essence, they are not overtly negatives but opportunities in disguise. Perceiving them as lessons learned can make a significant difference in your approach towards growth and improvement.

With an open mind and heart, equipped with the right tools and strategies, tracking your growth journey can be an enlightening experience. It's a process that breeds acknowledgment, self-awareness, and success. With each step measured and each mile marked, you're not only moving closer to your goals, you're becoming a more aware, more resilient version of yourself on this transformative journey.

Chapter 10. Cultivating Resilience in the Face of Adversity

As humans, we are undeniably prone to a kaleidoscope of experiences that span joy and sadness, triumph and failure, ease and adversity. These inevitable facets of the human condition serve as the paving stones on our path of growth, and among them — adversity plays a key, albeit challenging, role. Cultivating resilience in the face of adversity isn't a mere option but an essential life skill, a trait that ultimately determines whether we stagnate or evolve against the odds. This chapter aims to elucidate the nuances of resilience, and its importance, intertwined with practical methods to cultivate this robust trait.

10.1. The Essence of Resilience

Resilience is our innate strength, it empowers us to recover quickly from difficulties, adapt to change, and to keep going in the face of adversity. It is not a rare ability reserved for a select few; it is a set of behaviors, thoughts, and actions that can be learned and developed by anyone.

In reality, life isn't a perfectly laid out plan. It seldom goes the way we envision it, and the ability to cope effectively with the unexpected trials and tribulations is what separates the resilient from the rest. It is a scaffolding upon which our ability to navigate life's tumultuous winds and terrific storms is built.

10.2. Understanding Adversity

Before we delve into the intricacies of cultivating resilience, it is crucial to understand what adversity actually encompasses. Adversity, in simplest terms, is hardship or an adverse event or circumstance. It can be tangible, such as loss of a job or failure in a test or more abstract, like a fallout with a loved one or a crisis of faith. It might be brief, or it could last for a prolonged spell of time. Adversity, being subjective, varies in its magnitude and gravity.

The point of this discussion isn't to distress you, rather it is to emphasize the fact that adversity isn't just for the unluckily chosen; it is a ubiquitous part of the human experience. Sooner or later, it arrives at every doorstep. The key to weathering these episodes is to cultivate resilience.

10.3. Ways to Cultivate Resilience

Building resilience is an active process, requiring conscious effort, time, and dedication. It should not be perceived as a quick-fix solution, but as a journey of self-improvement. Here are the ways we can cultivate resilience.

1. Embrace Change: Change is constant. Learning to accept and adapt to the different phases of life forms the core of resilience.

2. Cultivate Optimism: A positive mindset can act as a buffer against stress. This doesn't mean ignoring the problem, but approaching hardships with a more positive and productive outlook.

3. Develop Problem-Solving Skills: Enhancing your ability to solve problems efficiently and proactively aids in cultivating resilience.

4. Foster Strong Relationships: Building strong, positive relationships with loved ones can provide you with the necessary support and encouragement needed during challenging times.

5. Find Your Purpose: Knowing what you're striving for can provide a sense of direction and motivation during trying times.

6. Take Care of Your Physical Health: Regular exercise, a healthy

diet, adequate sleep – all influence your capacity to cope with stress and adversity.

7. Seek Professional Help: If you're struggling to cope with adversity, reaching out to a mental health professional can be immensely beneficial.

10.4. Resilience Isn't About Going It Alone

While resilience is inherently a personal trait, its cultivation doesn't imply an isolated battle against adversity. In fact, the importance of robust support systems cannot be understated. In moments of adversity, reaching out for help is a strength, not a weakness. You could seek assistance from friends, family, mentors, counseling professionals, and support groups, to name a few. A support network provides both emotional and practical assistance, creating an environment conducive to nurturing resilience.

10.5. Growing through Adversity

The phenomenon of post-traumatic growth elucidates how adversity, when viewed through the lens of resilience, can lead to significant personal growth. People who endure adversity and struggle can often build resilience and even emerge stronger having learned from their experiences, refining their perspectives and reinforcing their values.

In conclusion, cultivating resilience in the face of adversity is not about evading hardships, but about formulating strategies to ride the waves. With resilience, you will not just confront adversity head-on, but also learn and grow from it, multiplying your growth potential endless fold. When life pushes you down seven times, resilience inspires you to stand up eight. With this empowering attribute embedded in your toolkit, the capricious winds of adversity will only fan the flames of your relentless pursuit of growth.

Chapter 11. The Future of Growth: Anticipating and Preparing for Change

In the relentless pursuit of growth, it is crucial to cast a revisionary gaze upon what the future holds; for in its understanding lie the keys to not just survival, but thriving amidst inevitable change. The grand canvas of future envisions a landscape that is as uncertain as it is promising, opening up new avenues for growth and unparalleled opportunities as well as colossal challenges. The fast-paced world we live in is characterized by an ever-evolving economy, drastic shifts in technology, social and cultural upheavals, and frequent variances in public policy. Any strategy aimed at personal or professional growth that overlooks this dynamism risks being rendered futile, or worse, counterproductive. Thereby, like the expert chess player who always stays several moves ahead, we also need to anticipate and prepare for the future of growth.

11.1. Decoding the Future: Understanding the Context

The task of predicting the future is, undisputedly, an arduous one. This task is juxtaposed with myriad variables that shift and alter with a dizzying alacrity, all contributing to rendering a firm grasp of it an equivalent of building castles in the air. Yet, understanding these variables and recognizing patterns in their behavior is central to framing our growth narrative. The first step towards this is gaining an intellectual awareness of the factors that shape our future society and the world at large.

These factors could range from the macroeconomic, such as market trends, global economics, population dynamics and climate change, to individual-driven aspects like consumption patterns, lifestyle preferences and attitudinal shifts. Grasping this labyrinth of elements is comparable to holding a magnifying lens to the world, enabling us to see the granular details and make sense of what may seem random at first glance. It underscores the importance of continuous learning to remain updated and relevant, a point iterated throughout this report.

11.2. Playing the Long Game: Creating a Future-Ready Blueprint

Once we have developed a reasonable understanding of the context, the task shifts towards how we can constructively use this knowledge to stimulate our growth journey. Enter the Future-Ready Blueprint, an undeniable cornerstone for anyone striving for unceasing improvement. It is a strategic framework, derived from the understanding of the future context, which outlines the essential abilities, skills, and attitudes that will need to be developed and refined to negotiate effectively with the upcoming challenges and adapt to the winds of change.

The contents of this blueprint will vary greatly for each person, as variables such as personal aptitude, professional field, societal milieu and individual aspirations come into play. However, some key elements remain consistent such as adaptability, resilience, continuous learning, creativity and a proactive mindset. This blueprint, in essence, equips us with an actionable roadmap for our own growth story as we navigate through the unpredictable landscape of the future.

11.3. Embracing Change: The Imperative

Change, a constant companion in our journey of growth, often arrives in waves, reshaping the topography of our lives and careers. While the instinctual response to change is resistance, growth seekers understand that adapting to change, rather than resisting it, propels progress. Harnessing the power of change necessitates an attitudinal shift from viewing it as an obstacle to accepting it as an engine of growth.

Every era heralds significant shifts in technology, culture, economy and society, and with these shifts come abundant opportunities for growth. Remaining dedicated to continuous learning, nurturing creativity, and fostering resilience can help ride these waves of change with confidence and grace. This section underlines the importance of cultivating these key attributes to remain agile, versatile and adaptable in a swiftly changing world.

In the quest for constant growth, what stands between the present and the future isn't simply a passage of time, but a courage-fueled journey, steered by a relentless pursuit of learning, accepting, adapting and improving. By cultivating these qualities and embracing the future, we set ourselves on a destined path of lifelong learning and upgrade, thus inculcating a paradigm that views growth as an evolving continuum, not a finite destination.